CELEBRATING THE NAME ASHLEY

Celebrating the Name Ashley

Walter the Educator

SKB
Silent King Books

dedicated to everyone with the first
name of Ashley

ASHLEY

In a world of wonder and delight,

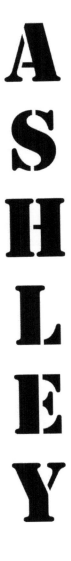

There shines a name so pure and bright,

Ashley, a name like a melody,

A symphony of grace and harmony.

From ancient roots with meaning deep,

Ashley, a name that will forever keep,

A legacy of beauty and strength,

A name that goes to any length.

In the gardens of life, Ashley blooms,

Spreading joy and banishing glooms,

A beacon of hope in darkened days,

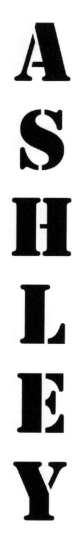

Guiding with wisdom in countless ways.

In the tapestry of time, Ashley's thread,

Weaves a story that's never been said,

A tale of courage and fierce determination,

A name that echoes through every nation.

In the realm of art, Ashley's muse,

Inspiring creativity with nothing to lose,

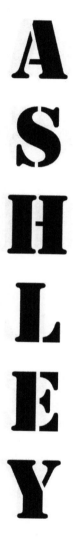

A canvas of dreams, a sculpture of passion,

A name that fuels the fire of imagination.

In the dance of love, Ashley's embrace,

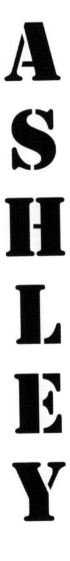

A tender touch, a gentle grace,

A
S
H
L
E
Y

A heart that beats with endless affection,

A name that ignites the flames of connection.

In the realm of nature, Ashley's song,

A melody that's pure and strong,

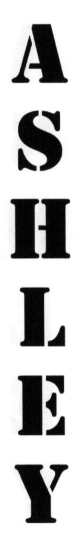

A voice that echoes through the trees,

A name that dances on every breeze.

In the corridors of power, Ashley stands,

A force to be reckoned with in every land,

A leader with vision and unwavering might,

A name that commands respect day and night.

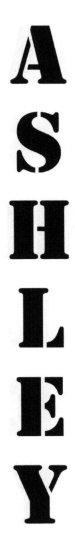

In the symphony of life, Ashley's tune,

A melody that's never out of tune,

A rhythm that pulses with boundless energy,

A name that embodies true synergy.

In the tapestry of humanity, Ashley's thread,

A unique masterpiece, never to be misread,

A name that shines in every single hue,

A
S
H
L
E
Y

A name that's simply and beautifully you.

ABOUT THE CREATOR

Walter the Educator is one of the pseudonyms for Walter Anderson. Formally educated in Chemistry, Business, and Education, he is an educator, an author, a diverse entrepreneur, and he is the son of a disabled war veteran. "Walter the Educator" shares his time between educating and creating. He holds interests and owns several creative projects that entertain, enlighten, enhance, and educate, hoping to inspire and motivate you.

Follow, find new works, and stay up to date with Walter the Educator™ at WaltertheEducator.com

Milton Keynes UK
Ingram Content Group UK Ltd.
UKHW020638040324
438885UK00016B/800

9 798869 211934